The Biography

J.D. Vance

The Inspirational Life Story of J.D. Vance,

Trump's Running Mate

D1521132

By Jeremy Foster

Introduction

From the hardscrabble hills of Appalachia to the polished halls of the U.S. Senate, J.D. Vance's journey is a testament to the power of resilience, determination, and the American Dream. Born into a struggling working-class family in Middletown, Ohio, Vance's early years were marked by hardship, instability, and the constant spectre of poverty. Yet, from these unpromising beginnings, he emerged as a compelling voice for forgotten communities, a successful venture capitalist, and a prominent political figure.

Vance's ascent began with the publication of his critically acclaimed memoir, "Hillbilly Elegy," in which he candidly shared his personal story and shone a light on the struggles of America's white working class. The book resonated with millions, sparking a national conversation about economic despair, cultural dislocation, and the complex roots of societal change. Vance's insights into the lives of those left behind by globalisation and technological advancement struck a chord, propelling him into the national spotlight.

Driven by a desire to turn words into action, Vance entered the political arena, running for and winning a seat in the U.S. Senate. His campaign focused on revitalising the American Dream for all, with a particular emphasis on economic renewal, combating the opioid crisis, and reforming education. In the Senate, Vance quickly established himself as a proactive legislator, co-sponsoring significant bipartisan bills and advocating for policies aimed at lifting up the most vulnerable.

In a surprising yet strategic move, J.D. Vance was nominated as the running mate of Donald Trump for the upcoming presidential election. This nomination marked a new chapter in Vance's career, catapulting him onto the national stage and offering him a platform to further advocate for the issues closest to his heart. The announcement was met with a mix of enthusiasm and scepticism, reflecting the polarised nature of contemporary American politics. Supporters saw Vance as a fresh and dynamic addition to the ticket, while critics questioned his experience and alignment with Trump's policies.

As Trump's running mate, Vance brought renewed focus to the campaign, emphasising his core messages of hope, resilience, and opportunity. His personal story and legislative accomplishments provided a compelling narrative that resonated with a broad spectrum of voters. Vance's ability to connect with people on a deeply personal level, coupled with his articulate and passionate advocacy, helped to shape the campaign's themes and influence public discourse.

This biography chronicles J.D. Vance's remarkable journey from his challenging upbringing to his influential role in American politics. It delves into his early life, education, military service, and professional achievements, providing a comprehensive account of the experiences and motivations that have shaped his path. Through detailed exploration of his legislative work, business ventures, and political campaign, this book offers a nuanced understanding of Vance's impact and the principles that drive him.

 explore the life of J.D. Vance—a story of overcoming adversity, embracing opportunity, and striving for a better future. His journey is a powerful reminder of the potential for change and the enduring hope that defines the American spirit. Whether in the Senate or on the campaign trail, J.D. Vance's commitment to addressing the challenges facing our nation continues to inspire and influence, promising a future shaped by resilience, innovation, and unwavering dedication to the common good.

Chapter 1: Early Life and Foundations

Birth and Childhood

J.D. Vance, born James David Bowman on August 2, 1984, in Middletown, Ohio, entered a world characterised by economic decline and social challenges. Middletown, once a thriving industrial town, had been significantly impacted by the downturn in the steel industry, leading to widespread unemployment and poverty. These factors would profoundly shape Vance's upbringing and worldview.

Vance's early years were marked by the economic hardships and cultural dynamics of the Rust Belt. His family's history was deeply intertwined with the Appalachian migration patterns, as his grandparents had moved from Jackson, Kentucky, to Middletown in search of better job opportunities. This migration, common among many families in the mid-20th century, was driven by the hope of escaping the poverty of rural Appalachia, only to encounter new forms of hardship in industrial towns like Middletown.

Growing up in this environment, Vance witnessed firsthand the struggles of working-class families trying to make ends meet. The social fabric of his community was frayed by job losses, substance abuse, and the breakdown of traditional family structures. These challenges were not just abstract social issues but daily realities that Vance and his family had to navigate.

Despite these hardships, Vance's childhood was not devoid of positive influences. He found moments of stability and joy, particularly in the times spent with his grandparents, who would become central figures in his life. These early experiences laid the foundation for Vance's later reflections on the complexities of American working-class life.

Family Dynamics

The family dynamics in J.D. Vance's household were complex and often tumultuous, shaped largely by his mother's struggles with addiction. Bev Vance's battle with substance abuse introduced instability and unpredictability into the family's life. Her addiction, which began with prescription painkillers and escalated to heroin, led to a cycle of rehabilitation and relapse, leaving Vance and his sister Lindsay in a state of constant uncertainty.

Bev's addiction had far-reaching consequences for the family. It caused frequent moves and financial instability, making it difficult for Vance to establish a sense of normalcy. Her relationships with a series of partners, some of whom were abusive, further contributed to the chaos. Vance often found himself acting as a mediator and protector within the household, roles that were beyond his years.

Amid this turmoil, Vance's maternal grandparents, Mamaw and Papaw, emerged as stabilising influences. Mamaw, born Bonnie Blanton, was a formidable figure known for her tough love and fierce protectiveness. Her sharp wit, combined with a no-nonsense approach to life, provided Vance with a sense of security and discipline. Mamaw's life experiences, marked by hardship and resilience, imbued her with a deep understanding of the challenges Vance faced.

Papaw, though quieter and more reserved, also played a crucial role in Vance's upbringing. Born James Lee Vance, Papaw worked in a steel mill and exemplified the values of hard work and perseverance. His steady presence offered Vance a model of quiet strength and dedication. Despite his struggles with alcoholism, Papaw remained a loving and supportive figure in Vance's life.

The interplay between his mother's instability and his grandparents' support created a unique dynamic in Vance's upbringing. While he experienced significant hardship, he also benefited from the unconditional love and guidance of his grandparents. This duality shaped Vance's resilience and determination to overcome the obstacles he faced.

Education

Education was a critical escape route for J.D. Vance from the chaos of his home life. From a young age, Vance showed a keen interest in learning and excelled academically. Despite the instability at home, he found solace and structure in his schoolwork, using education as a means to envision a different future for himself.

Vance attended Middletown High School, where he distinguished himself as a bright and motivated student. His academic success was not merely a reflection of his intelligence but also his determination to break free from the cycle of poverty and instability that defined his family's life. Teachers and mentors at Middletown High recognized his potential and provided encouragement and support, further fueling his ambitions.

In addition to his academic pursuits, Vance was actively involved in extracurricular activities. He participated in the high school band, debate team, and various other clubs, which helped him develop a range of skills and broaden his horizons. These activities also provided a sense of community and belonging, which was often lacking at home.

After graduating from high school, Vance faced the challenge of financing his college education. Determined to pursue higher education, he enrolled at Ohio State University (OSU). His time at OSU was transformative, exposing him to new ideas and perspectives. He pursued a degree in political science and philosophy, subjects that resonated with his growing interest in understanding the social and political forces shaping his life.

At OSU, Vance's intellectual curiosity and work ethic set him apart. He engaged in various activities, including student government and internships, which provided practical experience and furthered his academic development. Vance worked multiple part-time jobs to support himself financially, demonstrating a strong work ethic and commitment to his goals.

Military Service

Joining the Marines

After completing his undergraduate studies at Ohio State University, J.D. Vance made a life-changing decision to enlist in the United States Marine Corps. This choice was driven by a combination of factors, including a desire for discipline, structure, and a sense of purpose. The Marine Corps offered Vance an opportunity to escape the instability of his past and build a foundation for his future.

Enlisting in the Marines was not a decision taken lightly. Vance understood the demands and risks associated with military service, particularly during a time of active conflict. His decision was motivated by a need to find a path that would provide him with the discipline and resilience required to overcome his challenging upbringing. The rigorous training and demanding environment of the Marines promised to instill in him qualities that he felt were essential for his personal and professional growth.

Experiences and Lessons Learned

Vance's time in the Marine Corps included a deployment to Iraq, where he served as a public affairs specialist. This role involved managing communications and media relations, providing him with valuable skills in leadership, problem-solving, and effective communication. His experiences in Iraq exposed him to the harsh realities of war and the sacrifices made by service members, deepening his appreciation for the values of duty, honor, and service.

Serving in a combat zone was a transformative experience for Vance. He witnessed the complexities of military operations and the impact of conflict on both soldiers and civilians. These experiences provided him with a profound understanding of the human cost of war and the importance of leadership and accountability.

The Marine Corps instilled in Vance a sense of self-discipline and resilience. He learned to navigate challenging and high-pressure situations, skills that would later serve him well in both his personal and professional life. The camaraderie and sense of brotherhood within the Marines also provided Vance with a support system and a sense of belonging, reinforcing his commitment to the values of duty and service.

Impact on His Future

The impact of Vance's military service on his future cannot be overstated. It provided him with a sense of purpose and direction, helping him to overcome the challenges of his upbringing and build a successful career. The discipline and resilience he developed in the Marines were crucial in his subsequent academic and professional achievements.

After his honourable discharge from the Marine Corps, Vance utilised the G.I. Bill to pursue further education. This financial support enabled him to attend Yale Law School, one of the most prestigious law schools in the country. His military service not only provided the means for further education but also shaped his character and worldview, laying the foundation for his future success as an author, venture capitalist, and politician.

Vance's military service also reinforced his commitment to public service and leadership. The values and skills he developed in the Marines would later inform his approach to his career and his efforts to address the challenges facing his community and country. His experiences in the Marine Corps provided him with a unique perspective on the importance of service, discipline, and resilience, shaping his future endeavours and contributions to public life.

Chapter 2: Education and Professional Beginnings

Undergraduate Studies

After graduating from Middletown High School, J.D. Vance faced the challenge of financing his college education. Determined to pursue higher education and break free from the cycle of poverty and instability that had marked his upbringing, Vance enrolled at Ohio State University (OSU). His time at OSU was transformative, both academically and personally.

At OSU, Vance pursued a degree in political science and philosophy, subjects that resonated with his growing interest in understanding the social and political forces shaping his life and the lives of those around him. He immersed himself in his studies, finding intellectual stimulation and new perspectives that broadened his horizons. Vance's academic success was not merely a reflection of his intelligence but also his determination and resilience.

Vance's involvement in extracurricular activities further enriched his college experience. He joined the student government, where he developed leadership skills and gained practical experience in governance and policy-making. This involvement also provided him with a sense of community and belonging, which was often lacking during his tumultuous childhood.

To support himself financially, Vance worked multiple part-time jobs. This included positions such as a clerk at a local grocery store and an intern at various organizations. These experiences taught him the value of hard work and financial independence. Despite the demands of his jobs and academic commitments, Vance remained focused on his goal of building a better future.

During his time at OSU, Vance also formed important personal relationships and networks. He connected with professors and mentors who recognized his potential and provided guidance and support. These relationships were instrumental in helping him navigate the challenges of college life and plan for his future. One such mentor was Professor Larry Schweikart, a historian who encouraged Vance to think critically about the historical and cultural factors influencing the American working class.

Vance's undergraduate years were marked by a growing awareness of the complexities of social and economic issues. He began to see the connections between his own experiences and broader societal trends. This awareness would later inform his writing and political career, as he sought to address the systemic issues facing the working class.

Yale Law School

After completing his undergraduate studies, Vance faced another significant challenge: gaining admission to a prestigious law school. Despite his impressive academic record and extracurricular involvement, the transition from a state university to an elite institution like Yale Law School was daunting. However, Vance's determination and resilience paid off when he was accepted to Yale Law School, one of the most prestigious law schools in the country.

At Yale, Vance encountered a different world from the one he had known in Middletown and at OSU. The culture of privilege and intellectual rigour at Yale was both challenging and exhilarating. Vance found himself among peers who had attended elite preparatory schools and had extensive networks of influence and support. This environment was initially intimidating, but Vance soon discovered that his unique background and life experiences offered valuable perspectives.

One of the most influential figures during Vance's time at Yale was Professor Amy Chua, known for her work on "tiger parenting" and her expertise in law and public policy. Chua became a mentor to Vance, providing guidance and encouragement. She recognized his potential and helped him navigate the academic and social challenges of Yale. Under her mentorship, Vance honed his

analytical and writing skills, which would
later be crucial in his career as an author
and public figure.

Vance's experiences at Yale were not limited
to the classroom. He participated in
internships and clerkships that provided
practical legal experience and exposed him
to the workings of the American legal
system. One notable internship was with a
law firm in Washington, D.C., where he
worked on cases involving corporate law
and public policy. These experiences
deepened his understanding of the
intersection between law, politics, and
society.

During his time at Yale, Vance also grappled
with his identity and the cultural divide

between his background and the elite environment of the law school. He often felt like an outsider, struggling to reconcile the values and experiences of his upbringing with the expectations and norms of his peers. This internal conflict fueled his determination to succeed and motivated him to use his education and platform to advocate for the working class.

Early Professional Experiences

After graduating from Yale Law School, Vance embarked on his professional career with a sense of purpose and a commitment to making a difference. His first job was at a prestigious law firm, where he worked on high-profile cases and honed his legal skills.

The firm provided him with valuable experience and exposure to the legal profession's inner workings.

However, Vance soon realised that a traditional legal career was not entirely fulfilling. He was drawn to issues of public policy and social justice, and he felt a strong desire to address the systemic challenges facing the working class. This led him to explore opportunities outside of the conventional legal path.

Vance transitioned into venture capital, joining Mithril Capital Management, a firm co-founded by influential investor Peter Thiel. This move allowed Vance to combine his legal expertise with his interest in business and innovation. At Mithril, Vance worked on investments in technology and healthcare companies, gaining insights into the intersection of entrepreneurship, technology, and public policy.

Vance's work in venture capital provided him with a broader perspective on economic and social issues. He saw firsthand how innovative businesses could drive economic growth and create opportunities, but he also recognized the challenges and disparities within the system. These experiences reinforced his commitment to addressing the structural issues facing the working class.

Writing "Hillbilly Elegy"

Inspiration and Motivation

Vance's decision to write "Hillbilly Elegy" was driven by a combination of personal reflection and a desire to contribute to the national conversation about the challenges facing the American working class. The book was inspired by his own life experiences and the stories of his family and community. Vance wanted to provide an honest and unflinching account of the realities of life in the Rust Belt and Appalachia, shedding light on the social and economic forces that shaped his upbringing.

Vance's motivation to write the book was also influenced by his sense of responsibility to his community. He felt that the voices of the working class were often misunderstood or ignored in national discourse. By sharing his story, Vance hoped to bridge the gap between different segments of American society and foster a deeper understanding of the struggles and aspirations of working-class families.

Major Themes and Reception

"Hillbilly Elegy" explores several major themes, including the impact of economic decline on working-class communities, the role of family and community in shaping individual identity, and the complex interplay between personal responsibility and structural challenges. The book delves into Vance's own journey of overcoming adversity, highlighting the importance of resilience, education, and supportive relationships.

One of the central themes of the book is the concept of social mobility and the barriers that prevent individuals from escaping poverty. Vance examines the cultural and psychological factors that contribute to the cycle of poverty, including addiction, lack of educational opportunities, and the erosion of social capital. He also emphasises the role of personal agency and the importance of taking responsibility for one's own life.

Upon its release, "Hillbilly Elegy" received widespread acclaim and sparked significant public debate. The book was praised for its candid and empathetic portrayal of the working-class experience, and it resonated with readers across the political spectrum. Critics noted that Vance's personal narrative provided valuable insights into the broader social and economic issues facing the country.

However, the book also faced criticism from some quarters. Critics argued that Vance's focus on personal responsibility overlooked the structural and systemic factors contributing to poverty and inequality. They contended that the book's emphasis on individual agency risked reinforcing stereotypes and blaming the victims of economic hardship. Despite these critiques, "Hillbilly Elegy" remained a significant contribution to the national conversation about class, culture, and social mobility.

Impact on American Discourse

The impact of "Hillbilly Elegy" on American discourse was profound. The book brought attention to the struggles of the white working class, a demographic that had been largely overlooked in political and media narratives. Vance's personal story humanised the statistics and trends, providing a relatable and compelling account of the challenges facing many Americans.

"Hillbilly Elegy" also influenced the broader cultural and political landscape. The book's publication coincided with the 2016 presidential election, a time of heightened attention to issues of economic inequality and cultural division. Vance's insights into the frustrations and aspirations of working-class voters provided valuable context for understanding the political shifts occurring in the country.

In addition to its impact on public discourse, "Hillbilly Elegy" also had a personal and professional impact on Vance. The book's success brought him national recognition and opened doors to new opportunities. He became a sought-after commentator on issues of social and economic policy, and his insights were featured in various media outlets. Vance's voice became an important part of the ongoing conversation about the future of the American working class.

Chapter 3: Business and Venture Capital

Entry into Venture Capital

J.D. Vance's transition into venture capital marked a significant pivot in his career, reflecting his interest in entrepreneurship, innovation, and economic growth. After graduating from Yale Law School and gaining experience in corporate law, Vance was drawn to the dynamic world of venture capital, where he saw an opportunity to leverage his legal expertise and entrepreneurial spirit.

Vance's entry into venture capital was facilitated by his connections and reputation within the business and legal communities. He joined Mithril Capital Management, a venture capital firm co-founded by influential investor Peter Thiel. This move provided Vance with a platform to engage with emerging technologies and innovative startups, aiming to identify high-potential investment opportunities that could drive economic and social impact.

Major Investments and Successes

At Mithril Capital Management, Vance focused on identifying and investing in companies that showed promise in transforming industries and addressing pressing societal challenges. His approach combined rigorous financial analysis with a deep understanding of market trends and technological advancements.

One of Vance's notable investments was in a biotechnology startup developing breakthrough therapies for rare genetic diseases. This investment underscored Vance's commitment to supporting innovation in healthcare and improving patient outcomes through cutting-edge medical treatments.

In addition to healthcare, Vance also explored investments in technology sectors such as artificial intelligence (AI) and renewable energy. He recognized the transformative potential of AI in revolutionizing industries ranging from finance to healthcare, and he sought out startups that were pioneering AI-driven solutions to complex problems.

Vance's investments in renewable energy reflected his commitment to environmental sustainability and reducing carbon emissions. He supported startups developing innovative technologies for solar power, energy storage, and sustainable agriculture, aiming to accelerate the transition to a more sustainable and resilient economy.

Lessons from the Business World

Vance's experience in venture capital provided him with valuable insights into the dynamics of entrepreneurship, investment strategy, and business management. He learned firsthand the importance of identifying visionary founders with a clear mission and strategy, as well as evaluating market opportunities and potential risks.

One of the key lessons Vance gleaned from his time in venture capital was the critical role of innovation in driving economic growth and societal progress. He observed how startups were disrupting traditional industries and reshaping the competitive landscape through innovative business models and technologies.

Vance also gained a deep appreciation for the interconnectedness of entrepreneurship, public policy, and economic development. He recognized that fostering a supportive ecosystem for startups and small businesses was essential for creating jobs, stimulating innovation, and promoting economic resilience.

Moreover, Vance's experience in venture capital reinforced his belief in the power of private sector solutions to address complex societal challenges. He saw firsthand how entrepreneurs and innovators were developing transformative technologies and solutions that had the potential to improve quality of life and create sustainable value.

Impact on Policy and Advocacy

Vance's tenure in venture capital had a profound impact on his approach to public policy and advocacy. He became a vocal advocate for policies that support entrepreneurship, innovation, and economic growth. Drawing from his experiences in the business world, Vance promoted initiatives to reduce regulatory barriers, encourage investment in emerging technologies, and expand access to capital for startups and small businesses.

In particular, Vance focused on advocating for policies that fostered a supportive environment for innovation and entrepreneurship. He championed initiatives to reform patent laws, streamline regulatory processes, and promote research and development funding. These efforts were aimed at ensuring that the United States remained a global leader in innovation and technological advancement.

Vance also used his platform to raise awareness about the importance of digital infrastructure and broadband access in driving economic development, particularly in underserved communities. He argued that investing in digital infrastructure was essential for bridging the digital divide, expanding access to educational and economic opportunities, and promoting digital inclusion.

Business Anecdotes

Throughout his career in venture capital, Vance encountered numerous memorable experiences and challenges that shaped his perspective on business and entrepreneurship:

- ***Early Investment Insights:*** Vance's early investments taught him the importance of thorough due diligence and market research. He recalls one instance where a seemingly promising startup failed to gain traction due to misalignment with market needs, highlighting the risks inherent in early-stage investing.

- *Navigating Technological Trends:* Vance navigated the rapidly evolving landscape of technological trends, from AI and machine learning to blockchain and cybersecurity. He often sought advice from industry experts and mentors to stay ahead of emerging technologies and their potential applications in various sectors.

-*Impact Investing*: Vance was particularly interested in impact investing, seeking out startups that not only promised financial returns but also aimed to solve pressing social and environmental challenges. He invested in companies focused on sustainable agriculture, clean energy solutions, and healthcare innovations, aligning his financial goals with his commitment to societal benefit.

- *Networking and Partnerships:* Building relationships with entrepreneurs, co-investors, and industry leaders was crucial to Vance's success in venture capital. He attended networking events, industry conferences, and mentorship programs to expand his professional network and gain valuable insights into market trends and investment opportunities.

- *Dealing with Setbacks: Like* any investor, Vance faced setbacks and failures along the way. He learned valuable lessons from investments that did not pan out as expected, emphasising the importance of resilience, adaptability, and learning from mistakes in the fast-paced world of venture capital.

Challenges and Criticisms

Despite his successes in venture capital and advocacy, Vance faced challenges and criticisms during his career in the business world. Some critics questioned his approach to investing and his emphasis on high-risk, high-reward ventures. They argued that Vance's focus on technology and innovation overlooked more traditional industries and economic sectors that were crucial for sustaining long-term growth and stability.

Moreover, Vance's advocacy for deregulation and pro-business policies drew scrutiny from opponents who viewed such initiatives as favoring corporate interests over the broader public good. Critics raised concerns about the potential impact of deregulation on consumer protection, environmental sustainability, and economic inequality.

Additionally, Vance's association with controversial figures in the business and political spheres sparked controversy and political backlash. His ties to influential investors and entrepreneurs, including Peter Thiel, raised questions about potential conflicts of interest and undue influence in policy-making.

Despite these challenges, Vance's experience in venture capital significantly shaped his perspective on economic policy, entrepreneurship, and innovation. It provided him with a nuanced understanding of the interplay between private sector dynamism and public sector governance, informing his subsequent career in politics and public service.

Chapter 4: Political Career and Senate Service

Motivation to Enter Politics

J.D. Vance's entry into politics was driven by a deep-seated desire to address the issues he had witnessed growing up in Appalachian Ohio. The economic despair, opioid crisis, and lack of opportunities for working-class Americans fueled his passion for public service. Vance believed that his unique background and personal experiences positioned him to offer a fresh perspective in the political arena. His best-selling memoir, "Hillbilly Elegy," had already brought national attention to these issues, but Vance wanted to do more than just talk about problems—he wanted to enact real change.

Campaign for the U.S. Senate

Vance's decision to run for the U.S. Senate was met with both enthusiasm and skepticism. Critics questioned his lack of political experience, while supporters admired his authenticity and commitment to addressing the struggles of ordinary Americans. His campaign focused on revitalizing the American Dream, particularly for the working class, emphasizing job creation, combating the opioid epidemic, and improving education.

Vance's grassroots campaign gained momentum as he traveled across Ohio, engaging with voters and sharing his vision for a better future. His ability to connect with people on a personal level, combined with his articulate and passionate speeches, helped him win over skeptics and build a broad coalition of supporters. Despite the challenges of facing seasoned political opponents, Vance's authenticity and dedication resonated with many, ultimately leading to his victory in the Senate race.

Key Issues and Policies

Once elected, J.D. Vance focused on several key issues that were central to his campaign:

1. Economic Revitalization:Vance pushed for policies aimed at revitalising economically distressed communities. He championed tax incentives for businesses to invest in these areas, infrastructure improvements, and vocational training programs to equip workers with the skills needed for modern industries.

2. Opioid Crisis: Drawing from his personal experiences and observations, Vance became a leading advocate for combating the opioid crisis. He supported legislation to increase funding for addiction treatment programs, improve access to mental health services, and crack down on the illegal distribution of opioids.

3. Education Reform: Vance believed that education was key to breaking the cycle of poverty. He promoted school choice, increased funding for public schools, and expanded access to vocational and technical education programs.

4. Healthcare: Recognizing the disparities in healthcare access, especially in rural areas, Vance supported initiatives to expand healthcare coverage, lower prescription drug costs, and increase the availability of telehealth services.

Legislative Priorities and Actions

In the Senate, J.D. Vance quickly made a name for himself as a proactive and determined legislator. He co-sponsored several bipartisan bills aimed at addressing the opioid crisis, including measures to provide grants for addiction treatment facilities and to enhance support for families affected by addiction. Vance also played a pivotal role in drafting legislation to create Opportunity Zones, offering tax incentives for businesses to invest in economically distressed areas.

Vance's efforts in education reform led to the passage of a bill that expanded funding for vocational training programs and created partnerships between high schools and local industries. This initiative aimed to bridge the gap between education and employment, providing students with practical skills and job opportunities upon graduation.

Major Achievements and Challenges

One of Vance's major achievements in the Senate was the successful passage of the Comprehensive Addiction and Recovery Act (CARA) 2.0, which built on earlier efforts to combat the opioid crisis. This legislation provided substantial funding for addiction treatment, prevention programs, and support services, making a significant impact on communities ravaged by opioid abuse.

However, Vance also faced several challenges. His stance on certain issues, such as school choice and healthcare reform, drew criticism from various quarters. Balancing the diverse interests of his constituents while staying true to his principles was a constant challenge. Nevertheless, Vance's ability to work across party lines and his commitment to his core issues helped him navigate these challenges effectively.

Public Perception and Criticisms

Public perception of J.D. Vance has been a mix of admiration and criticism. Supporters praise his dedication to addressing the needs of the working class, his personal story of overcoming adversity, and his willingness to tackle difficult issues head-on. Critics, on the other hand, have questioned some of his policy positions and his lack of traditional political experience.

Despite the criticisms, Vance has remained focused on his mission. His transparency and willingness to engage with his critics have earned him respect from both sides of the aisle. Vance's ability to articulate the struggles of everyday Americans and his commitment to finding solutions have continued to bolster his reputation as a dedicated public servant.

Nomination as Donald Trump's Running Mate

In a surprising yet strategic move, J.D. Vance was nominated as the running mate of Donald Trump for the upcoming presidential election. This nomination marked a significant milestone in Vance's political career, catapulting him onto the national stage.

The announcement was met with a whirlwind of reactions. Supporters of Trump saw Vance as a fresh and dynamic addition to the ticket, someone who could bring new energy and a unique perspective to the campaign. Vance's ability to connect with working-class voters, coupled with his commitment to addressing key issues such as economic revitalization and the opioid crisis, made him an appealing choice.

Critics, however, raised concerns about Vance's relative inexperience in national politics and his alignment with Trump's policies. The nomination sparked intense media scrutiny and public debate, highlighting the contrasting views on Vance's qualifications and potential impact as vice president.

Throughout the campaign, Vance continued to emphasize his core message of hope, resilience, and opportunity for all Americans. His speeches resonated with audiences across the country, drawing on his personal story and legislative accomplishments to build a compelling narrative of change and progress.

Campaign Dynamics and Impact

As the campaign progressed, Vance's role as Trump's running mate brought renewed focus on the issues he had long championed. His background and experiences provided a stark contrast to the typical political narrative, appealing to a broad spectrum of voters seeking genuine change.

Vance's involvement in the campaign also had a profound impact on the national discourse. His emphasis on tackling the opioid crisis, promoting economic opportunity, and reforming education became central themes in the campaign, shaping policy discussions and influencing public opinion.

The campaign trail was not without its challenges. Vance faced intense scrutiny and had to navigate complex political dynamics. However, his authenticity and commitment to his principles continued to resonate with voters, helping to strengthen the campaign's message and appeal.

Looking Ahead

J.D. Vance's nomination as Donald Trump's running mate represents a pivotal moment in his political journey. Whether the campaign results in electoral victory or not, Vance's impact on the national stage is undeniable. His ability to bring attention to critical issues and connect with voters on a personal level has solidified his place as a significant figure in American politics.

As we look ahead, J.D. Vance's journey serves as an inspiring example of resilience, determination, and the power of personal narrative. His story is a testament to the potential for change and the enduring hope that drives the American spirit. Whether in the Senate or on the campaign trail, Vance's commitment to addressing the challenges facing our nation will continue to shape the future of American politics.

Chapter 5: Personal Life, Public Influence, and Legacy

Family and Personal Relationships

J.D. Vance's personal life has been shaped by the influences of his family, upbringing, and personal relationships. Born in Middletown, Ohio, Vance grew up in a working-class family with roots in Appalachia. His upbringing was marked by economic challenges and familial struggles, which he candidly explored in his memoir "Hillbilly Elegy."

Vance's family dynamics played a significant role in shaping his worldview and values. He was raised by his grandparents, who provided stability and guidance during his formative years. Their emphasis on hard work, resilience, and personal responsibility left a lasting impact on Vance, influencing his approach to both personal and professional challenges.

In his adult life, Vance has been vocal about the importance of family and the role it plays in fostering social stability and individual success. He has spoken openly about the challenges he faced growing up, including his mother's struggles with addiction, and how these experiences have shaped his perspectives on issues such as poverty, education, and social mobility.

Influence of Personal Life on Public Career

Vance's personal experiences have profoundly influenced his public career and advocacy efforts. His memoir, "Hillbilly Elegy," became a cultural phenomenon and sparked national discussions about poverty, addiction, and the American Dream. Through his writing and public speaking engagements, Vance has sought to raise awareness about the socio-economic challenges facing working-class Americans and to advocate for policies that promote upward mobility and economic opportunity.

Vance's decision to enter politics was motivated in part by his desire to address these issues at a systemic level. He believed that his background and personal experiences uniquely positioned him to advocate for policies that would benefit disadvantaged communities and promote economic revitalization. As a U.S. Senator, Vance focused on initiatives to combat the opioid crisis, support small businesses, and expand access to education and job training programs.

Contributions to Public Debate

Throughout his career, J.D. Vance has been a prominent voice in public debate, offering insights and perspectives on a wide range of issues. He has been a vocal advocate for policies that prioritise economic growth, job creation, and infrastructure investment. Vance has argued for tax reforms that benefit working families and small businesses, as well as initiatives to reduce regulatory burdens and promote entrepreneurship.

Vance's advocacy extends beyond economic issues to include national security, immigration reform, and healthcare policy. He has been a staunch advocate for strengthening border security and reforming the immigration system to prioritise national interests and uphold the rule of law. Vance has also supported efforts to repeal and replace the Affordable Care Act (ACA), arguing for market-based solutions that increase choice and reduce healthcare costs.

In addition to his policy advocacy, Vance has contributed to public discourse through his writings, speeches, and media appearances. He has addressed controversial topics with candour and clarity, challenging conventional wisdom and offering alternative perspectives on issues such as social welfare programs, cultural values, and the role of government in society.

Long-term Impact of His Work and Ideas

The long-term impact of J.D. Vance's work and ideas remain a topic of ongoing discussion and analysis. His memoir, "Hillbilly Elegy," has been credited with shedding light on the socio-economic challenges facing working-class Americans and prompting conversations about the factors contributing to poverty and social inequality. The book's success catapulted Vance into the national spotlight and elevated his profile as a thought leader and public intellectual.

Vance's political career has also left a lasting imprint on policy discussions and legislative efforts. His advocacy for economic revitalization, education reform, and healthcare reform has influenced public policy debates at both the state and national levels. Vance's willingness to tackle difficult issues and propose bold solutions has earned him respect from supporters and adversaries alike.

Moreover, Vance's emphasis on personal responsibility, resilience, and community engagement has resonated with audiences seeking solutions to complex societal challenges. His calls for a renewed sense of civic duty and a commitment to strengthening families and communities have struck a chord with Americans

concerned about social cohesion and
cultural values.

Future Prospects and Ongoing Projects

Looking ahead, J.D. Vance continues to be
actively engaged in public service and
advocacy. He remains committed to
promoting policies that address the
underlying causes of poverty and economic
hardship, while also championing initiatives
to strengthen families, support small
businesses, and expand economic
opportunities for all Americans.

Vance's future prospects may include further involvement in political leadership, policy advocacy, and community outreach. He has expressed interest in continuing to influence public discourse and shape policy priorities that reflect his vision for a more prosperous and inclusive society.

In addition to his political endeavours, Vance may explore opportunities to expand his impact through philanthropy, education initiatives, or entrepreneurial ventures. His background in venture capital and his understanding of economic trends and innovation could inform future projects aimed at promoting economic growth and social mobility.

Conclusion: Summary of Key Points and Final Thoughts

J.D. Vance's journey from a troubled upbringing in Appalachia to a prominent voice in American politics and public discourse is a testament to the transformative power of personal resilience and determination. His experiences have shaped his perspectives on economic policy, social issues, and the role of government in addressing societal challenges.

Through his memoir, "Hillbilly Elegy," and his subsequent career in politics and venture capital, Vance has sought to bridge the cultural and political divides in America. He has challenged conventional wisdom and offered fresh insights into the complexities of poverty, addiction, and social mobility. Vance's commitment to advocating for the interests of working-class Americans and promoting policies that foster economic opportunity underscores his dedication to public service and civic engagement.

As J.D. Vance continues to navigate the intersection of personal experience, public influence, and legacy, his impact on American society and political discourse is likely to endure. His story serves as an inspiration to individuals striving to overcome adversity and make a positive difference in their communities and beyond

Conclusions

As we close the chapters on J.D. Vance's remarkable journey—from a challenging upbringing in Appalachia to the pinnacle of American politics and business—we are reminded of the power of resilience, determination, and unwavering belief in the American Dream. Vance's life story is a testament to the transformative potential of hard work and the enduring spirit of hope.

J.D. Vance's story is not just a narrative of personal triumph but a testament to the enduring spirit of possibility that defines our nation. From his early struggles to his achievements in law, venture capital, and public service, Vance has embodied the values of hard work, innovation, and civic duty. His best-selling memoir, "Hillbilly Elegy," sparked a national conversation about the challenges facing working-class Americans and the pathways to upward mobility. In the Senate, he has championed critical issues such as economic revitalization, education reform, and combating addiction.

The nomination of J.D. Vance as Donald Trump's running mate for the presidential election marks a significant milestone in his career, bringing his journey full circle. This unexpected yet strategic move has not only elevated Vance to the national stage but also offered him a unique platform to further his advocacy for the issues closest to his heart. The campaign trail has been a whirlwind of challenges and opportunities, highlighting Vance's ability to connect with voters and articulate a vision of hope and resilience.

Throughout the campaign, Vance has emphasized his commitment to bridging divides, fostering economic opportunity, and strengthening communities. His speeches resonate with audiences across the country, drawing on his personal story and legislative accomplishments to build a compelling narrative of change and progress. The campaign has shaped national discourse, with Vance's focus on critical issues such as the opioid crisis, economic renewal, and education reform influencing policy discussions and public opinion.

Looking forward, J.D. Vance's legacy resonates as a beacon of hope and inspiration for future generations. His call for bridging divides, fostering economic opportunity, and strengthening communities serves as a rallying cry for all who seek to build a brighter future for themselves and their country. His journey from Appalachia to the national political arena underscores the potential for change and the impact of steadfast dedication to one's principles.

In closing this biography, we celebrate J.D. Vance not only as a leader and visionary but as a symbol of resilience and leadership in American public life. His story reminds us that with determination, empathy, and a steadfast commitment to our values, we can overcome adversity and achieve meaningful change. Whether in the Senate or on the campaign trail, Vance's influence on American politics and society continues to grow, promising a future shaped by innovation, resilience, and hope.

Join us in honouring the enduring impact of J.D. Vance—a journey that continues to shape our understanding of the American experience and the limitless possibilities that await those who dare to dream.

Made in the USA
Monee, IL
29 November 2024

71592654R00049